Breaking Lorca: Fourteen Poems of Love and Death

Larry Sawyer

Breaking Lorca: Fourteen Poems of Love and Death
by Larry Sawyer

ISBN: 978-1-304-82018-1

White Hole Press
Chicago, Illinois

Foreword

My first encounter with the poetry of Federico García Lorca occurred in a dark library as a teen in Fairborn, Ohio. Reading his poem "Romance Sonámbulo" for the first time was one of the genuine joys of my life, and this work is partially the reason why I began writing poetry. Like many, I also became fascinated recently with Walter White's descent into crime on AMC's television show *Breaking Bad.* Something halfway through the series made me think that the blood and violence and dark themes inherent in the show reminded me of the stark imagery in Lorca's poetry and this project began to be realized. It was exciting to place these characters into the new context of Lorca's work but I also spooked myself a bit while doing so. It was nearly an uneasy feeling to see how neatly the themes from the television show could live and breathe inside Lorca's poetry, which is a testament to the timelessness of Lorca's work. The reader is invited to compare these new poems to the originals to see how they were shape-shifted by the New Mexico sands.

—Larry Sawyer

The poems by Federico García Lorca upon which this book is based were translated by A. S. Kline: "Ballad of the Small Plaza," "Song of the Rider," "It's True," "Song of the Barren Orange Tree," "The Moon Wakes," "Farewell," Romance de la Luna, Luna," "Romance Sonámbulo," "The Unfaithful Wife," "Gacela of Unexpected Love," "Casida de la Rosa," "Casida of the Dark Doves," "Ay voz secreta del amor oscuro!," and "Every Song."

Ballad of the Small Molecule

Singing of children
in the high school silence:
Light of the flame, and
calm of the crystal!

THE CHILDREN

What does your pocket hold,
in its denim madness?

MYSELF

A peal from the life clock,
The chemistry of that darkness.

THE CHILDREN

You leave us cooking
in the smallest apartment.
Light of the isomers, and
stench of the buckets!

What do *you* burn with
your hands black with phosphine?

MYSELF

A rose made of cancer, and
a lily of whiteness.

THE CHILDREN

Rinse them in acid
Glassware of the ages.
Light of the burner, and
calm of the crystal!

What does your tongue feel,
scarlet and thirsting?

MYSELF

A taste of the worry
of my shaven forehead.

THE CHILDREN

Drink the heavy water
of the racing hearts of the ages.
Light of the blowtorch, and
arrhythmia of the accountant!

Why do you roam far
from the desert, RV?

MYSELF

I gave them grey matter
and found a Hank Schrader.

THE CHILDREN

Who showed you the road there,
made of protons and nuclei?

MYSELF

The fount and the stream of
the carwash of the ages.

THE CHILDREN

Do you go far from
elementary compounds?

MYSELF

Skyler filled with light, is
the mass of my heart, and
my classroom, so lost,
with bills and diagnoses,
and I will go far off,
behind those desert hills there,
cook close to the starlight,
to ask of the child there:
O, return me
my hope, my blue magic,
ripening like glass,
with a gas mask of feathers,
and a sword of blue product.

THE CHILDREN

You leave us begging, yo
in the shopping mall.

Lighting up the night,
cooking *your* crystal!

Enormous pupils
of parched ex-students
line up for that crystal,
light their own futures.

Song of the Partner

Albuquerque.
Far away, and lonely.

Full moon, dark camper,
lighter in my pocket.
Though I know all the desert roadways
I'll never get home.

Through the cacti, through the valley,
red phosphorous moon, a stalled RV.
Death looks right through me
from a suburb of Albuquerque.

Yo, how long the road is!
Yo, my stalled RV!
Death waits like a doormat for me,
in the desert outside Albuquerque.

Albuquerque.
Far away, and corny.

It’s True

Skyler, the pain it costs me
to love you as I love you!

For love of you, the air, it hurts,
and my heart,
and my hat, they hurt me.

Who would buy it from me? Saul?
This beaker I am holding,
and this sadness, consisting partly of a less-desired
levomethamphetamine isomer,
dressed in a Hazmat suit—for making love?

Ay, the dopamine it costs me
to love you as I love you!

Song of the Badger

C'mon Jesse. Cut
me some slack, yo.
Cut out my shadow.
Free me from the torture
of another day on *Grand Theft Auto.*

Why was I born among bros?
The daylight doesn't revolve around narcos.
And the night herself repeats *5-0*
in all her constellations.

I want to live *not* tied to Skinny Pete.
I shall dream that mad stacks of green
change inside my dreaming
into half-pound combo burritos.

Jesse, c'mon.
Be my Vader, yo.
Cut out my shadow.
Free me from the torture
of seeing myself stone broke.

When Saul Wakes

When his Caddy sails out
cash registers fade into stillness
and there commences 1,000 bat mitzvahs
that cannot be penetrated.

When Saul sails out
a strip mall hides earth's surface,
the heart feels like an island
in that infinite litigation.

Nobody ever ate a gyro
with such reckless abandon.
It is correct then,
to offer *two* to Huell.

When Saul bails you out
with a hundred crisp Benjamins,
your last coin made of silver
sobs in your pocket.

Farewell

If I am dying,
leave the patio door open.

Our child is eating a first orange.
(But from the RV, I cannot see her.)

Hank is reading *Leaves of Grass.*
(From my bedroom, I can hear him.)

If I am dying,
leave the patio door open.

Romance de la Luna, Gus

The moon comes from Mexico,
in her creamy-white petticoat.
Pinkman stares and stares.
The child is staring at her.
In the breeze, stirred,
a pink teddy bear falls from the sky
shows, pure and voluptuous,
an eye of blue crystal.

- 'Away, luna, luna, luna.
If the gypsies come here,
they'll take your heart for necklaces
and white rings.'- 'Child, let me dance now,'
says Gus. 'When the gypsies come here,
they'll find you on the anvil,
with your little eyes closed.'
- 'Away, luna, luna, luna,
because I hear their horses.'
- 'Child, go, but do not tread
on my blue crystalline empire.'

Tuco's riders come nearer
beating on the plain, drumming.
Inside the forge, the child cook
has both his eyes closed.

Through the desert they come,
Like thrown knives, their double assassins,
their heads held upright,
their half-open eyes.

Now Saul is calling.
Ay, he calls from the strip mall!
Through the lab goes the moon,
like a child's fingers gripping buckets.

In the desert DEA agents
are shouting and cursing.
The breeze guards, guards it.
The breeze guards all profit.

Romance Sonámbulo

"Dull, how I found it dull.
Dull wind. Dull branches.
Pinkman locked in a cage
and Heisenberg on the mountain."
With her waist that's made of shadow
Skyler dreams on the high veranda,
green the stash, and green the dresses,
with eyes of frozen silver.
Green, as I love you, greenly.
Beneath the moon run by Federales
surveillance cams look at her
things she cannot see.

Green, as I love you, greenly.
Great piles of green dollars
come with my husband in the shadows
open the basement and groan.
Holly's cries floating on the dawn wind
with the rasping of the branches,
and the mountain thieving cat-like
bristles with its sour graves.
Who is coming? And from where?
Skyler waits on the high veranda,
green the flesh and green the tresses,
dreaming of Mike the enforcer.

- 'Brother-in-law, friend, I want to barter
a plea bargain for your freedom,
sell my story to the *Inquirer*,
change my desk job for a promotion.
Brother mine, I come here bleeding
from the mountain pass of ambush.'
- 'If I could, my bald friend,
then maybe we'd strike a bargain,
but I am no longer I,

nor is this house, of mine, mine.'
- 'Brother-in-law, friend, I want to die now,
in my own bed watching television,
with Marie beside me, if she can be,
I mean if she isn't busy prying.
Can you see the wound I carry
from my throat to my heart?'
- 'Three hundred silver badges
your white shirt now carries.
Your blood stinks and oozes,
all around your cue ball head.
But I am no longer I,
nor is this house of mine, mine.'
- 'Let me then, at least, climb up there,
up towards the high verandas.
Let me climb, let me climb there,
up towards the green verandas.
High verandas of the moonlight,
where I hear the sound of waters.'

Now they climb, Heisenberg and Hank,
up there to the high veranda,
letting fall a trail of blood drops,
letting fall a trail of tears.
On the morning rooftops,
trembling, another Emmy.
A thousand tambourines of bluest glass
wound the light of daybreak. Green, as I love you,
greenly.

Green the wind, and green the money.
They climbed up, the two companions.
In the mouth, their dark plot lines
left there a strange flavor,
of gall, and mint, and sweet-basil.
- 'Brother, friend! Where is she, tell me,
where is she, your bitter Skyler?
How often, she waited for you!
How often, she would have waited,

cool the face, and bleach blonde the tresses,
on this green veranda!'

Over a new script's golden surface
Skyler deeply ponders.
Green *is* the flesh, green the tresses,
her eyes were frozen silver.
An ice-ray made of moonlight
held her above the water.
How intimate the night became,
as she thought of her alchemist husband and his cancer.
DEA agents were beating,
beating, beating on the door frame.
Green, as I love you, greenly.
Green the wind, and green the dollars.
Pinkman locked in a cage
and Heisenberg on the mountain.

The Unfaithful Wife

So I took her to the food court
operated on her like a surgeon,
but it seems she had a husband.
It was the night of the Albuquerque jazz fest,
and it almost was a *duty.*
The lamps went out,
the tits lit up.
By the last street corners
I touched her sleeping breasts,
and they suddenly had opened
like hyacinth petals or a sweet tax break.
The starch
of her slip crackled
in my ears like silk fragments
ripped apart by ten audits.
The tree crowns
free of silver light are larger,
and a horizon of dogs howls
far away from the river.
That's just how the Tedmeister rolls.

Past the hawthorns,
the reeds, and the brambles,
below her dome of hair
I made a hollow in the sand.
I took off my tie.
She took off a garment.
I my belt with my revolver.
She four bodices.
Creamy tuberoses
or shells are not as smooth as
her skin was, or, in the moonlight,
blue crystals shining brilliantly.
Damn, I looked good in my new BMW.

Her thighs slipped from me
like fish that are startled,
one half full of fire,
one half full of coldness.
That night I galloped
on the best of roadways,
on a mare of nacre,
without stirrups, without bridle.
I didn't even have my Blackberry *on* me.
That's how the Tedmeister rolls.
As a man I cannot tell you
the things she said to me.
The light of understanding
has made me most discreet.
Smeared with sand and kisses,
I took her from the river.
The blades of the lilies
were fighting with the air.

I behaved as what I am, proud
member of the Albuquerque Chamber of Commerce.
I gave her a job,
need some help with the filing.
I did not want to love her,
for though she has a dork husband,
chemistry teacher or something,
she said she was a virgin
when I took her to the river.

Jack of Unexpected Love

No one understands me
or the self-inflicted tattoos on my belly.
Who knew you ran a fucking car wash
or that Lydia was your Euro connection?

There slept a thousand little ex-cons
in the moonlit swastika of my forehead,
while, for four nights, I embraced there
Todd's shit product. (74%!)

Between the plaster and the jasmine,
your primo glass was a pale brunch, seeding.
I tried to give you a second chance, fucknut,
but you just had to try my patience.

Ever, ever: garden of my torture,
your blue product, flies from me forever,
the blood of your veins is in my mouth.
Now I'm going to get all Tuco on your ass.

Mike de la Rosa

Mike was
not looking for mourning:
on its branch, almost immortal,
he looked for something other.

He wasn't
looking for wisdom, or for shadow:
the edge of flesh and dreaming,
he looked for something other.

Mike was
not looking for the rose, was
unmoving in the heavens.
That brother just wanted to retire.

Todd of the Dark Doves

Through the laurel branches
Todd saw two doves of darkness.
The one it was the desert sun,
the other one was Lydia.
Lydia said: ‘Little lackey
where is my Splenda?’
‘In my tail-feathers,’ the sun said.
‘In my pants,’ said Todd.
And I who was out walking
with the earth wrapped round me,
saw two white supremacists,
and a girl who was naked.
And the one was the other,
and the girl, she was neither.
Lydia said: ‘Little Todd,
where is my shipment?’
‘In my tail-feathers,’ the sun said.
‘In my pants,’ said Todd.
Through the branches of laurel,
I realized just how stupid Todd is.
And the one was the other,
and the two of them were dead.

'Ay voz secreta del amor oscuro!'

O secret voice of hidden Whitmans!
O bleeding plot spoiler! O wound!
O dry poolside, bitter barbecue!
O uncertainty principle, mall-pocked city!

O night immense with Gustavo's pollo,
heavenly mountain, desert valley!
O Emmy inside the heart, future voiceovers for
endless car commercials, a full-blown bust!

Let me be, hot voice of all chili-dogs,
and do not ask me to vanish or dust
more file cabinets, where DEA are fruitless.

Leave my hard, ivory, bald, skull forever,
have pity on me. Stop the torture!
O I solved it, Heisenberg is so over!

Pinkman's Song

Every cook
is the remains
of love.

Every light
the remains
of time.
(A knot
of time, yo.)

And every sigh
the remains
of a high.

La familia es todo.

Ballad of the Small Plaza

Singing of children
in the night silence:
Light of the stream, and
calm of the fountain!

THE CHILDREN

What does your heart hold,
divine in its gladness?

MYSELF

A peal from the bell-tower,
lost in the dimness.

THE CHILDREN

You leave us singing
in the small plaza.
Light of the stream, and
calm of the fountain!

What do you hold in
your hands of springtime?

MYSELF

A rose of blood, and
a lily of whiteness.

THE CHILDREN

Dip them in water
of the song of the ages.
Light of the stream, and
calm of the fountain!

What does your tongue feel,
scarlet and thirsting?

MYSELF

A taste of the bones
of my giant forehead.

THE CHILDREN

Drink the still water
of the song of the ages.
Light of the stream, and
calm of the fountain!

Why do you roam far
from the small plaza?

MYSELF

I go to find Mages
and find princesses.

THE CHILDREN

Who showed you the road there,
the road of the poets?

MYSELF

The fount and the stream of
the song of the ages.

THE CHILDREN

Do you go far from
the earth and the ocean?

MYSELF

It’s filled with light, is
my heart of silk, and
with bells that are lost,

with bees and with lilies,
and I will go far off,
behind those hills there,
close to the starlight,
to ask of the Christ there
Lord, to return me
my child's soul, ancient,
ripened with legends,
with a cap of feathers,
and a sword of wood.

THE CHILDREN

You leave us singing
in the small plaza.
Light of the stream, and
calm of the fountain!

Enormous pupils
of the parched palm fronds
hurt by the wind, they
weep their dead leaves.

Song of the Rider

Córdoba.
Far away, and lonely.

Full moon, black pony,
olives against my saddle.
Though I know all the roadways
I'll never get to Córdoba.

Through the breezes, through the valley,
red moon, black pony.
Death is looking at me
from the towers of Córdoba.

Ay, how long the road is!
Ay, my brave pony!
Ay, death is waiting for me,
before I get to Córdoba.

Córdoba.
Far away, and lonely.

It's True

Ay, the pain it costs me
to love you as I love you!

For love of you, the air, it hurts,
and my heart,
and my hat, they hurt me.

Who would buy it from me,
this ribbon I am holding,
and this sadness of cotton,
white, for making handkerchiefs with?

Ay, the pain it costs me
to love you as I love you!

Song of the Barren Orange Tree

Woodcutter.
Cut out my shadow.
Free me from the torture
of seeing myself fruitless.

Why was I born among mirrors?
The daylight revolves around me.
And the night herself repeats me
in all her constellations.

I want to live not seeing self.
I shall dream the husks and insects
change inside my dreaming
into my birds and foliage.

Woodcutter.
Cut out my shadow.
Free me from the torture
of seeing myself fruitless.

The Moon Wakes

When the moon sails out
the bells fade into stillness
and there emerge the pathways
that can’t be penetrated.

When the moon sails out
the water hides earth’s surface,
the heart feels like an island
in the infinite silence.

Nobody eats an orange
under the moon’s fullness.
It is correct to eat, then,
green and icy fruit.

When the moon sails out
with a hundred identical faces,
the coins made of silver
sob in your pocket.

Farewell

If I am dying,
leave the balcony open.

The child is eating an orange.
(From my balcony, I see him.)

The reaper is reaping the barley.
(From my balcony, I hear him.)

If I am dying,
leave the balcony open.

Romance de la Luna, Luna

The moon comes to the forge,
in her creamy-white petticoat.
The child stares, stares.
The child is staring at her.
In the breeze, stirred,
the moon stirs her arms
shows, pure, voluptuous,
her breasts of hard tin.

- 'Away, luna, luna, luna.
If the gypsies come here,
they'll take your heart for
necklaces and white rings.'
- 'Child, let me dance now.
When the gypsies come here,
they'll find you on the anvil,
with your little eyes closed.'
- 'Away, luna, luna, luna,
because I hear their horses.'
- 'Child, go, but do not tread
on my starched whiteness.'

The riders are coming nearer
beating on the plain, drumming.
Inside the forge, the child
has both his eyes closed.

Through the olive trees they come,
bronze, and dream, the gypsies,
their heads held upright,
their eyes half-open.
How the owl is calling.
Ay, it calls in the branches!
Through the sky goes the moon,
gripping a child's fingers.

In the forge the gypsies
are shouting and weeping.
The breeze guards, guards.
The breeze guards it.

Romance Sonámbulo

Green, as I love you, greenly.
Green the wind, and green the branches.
The dark ship on the sea
and the horse on the mountain.
With her waist that's made of shadow
dreaming on the high veranda,
green the flesh, and green the tresses,
with eyes of frozen silver.
Green, as I love you, greenly.
Beneath the moon of the gypsies
silent things are looking at her
things she cannot see.

Green, as I love you, greenly.
Great stars of white hoarfrost
come with the fish of shadow
opening the road of morning.
The fig tree's rubbing on the dawn wind
with the rasping of its branches,
and the mountain thieving-cat-like
bristles with its sour agaves.
Who is coming? And from where...?
She waits on the high veranda,
green the flesh and green the tresses,

dreaming of the bitter ocean.

- 'Brother, friend, I want to barter
your house for my stallion,
sell my saddle for your mirror,
change my dagger for your blanket.
Brother mine, I come here bleeding
from the mountain pass of Cabra.'
- 'If I could, my young friend,
then maybe we'd strike a bargain,
but I am no longer I,
nor is this house, of mine, mine.'
- 'Brother, friend, I want to die now,
in the fitness of my own bed,
made of iron, if it can be,
with its sheets of finest cambric.
Can you see the wound I carry
from my throat to my heart?'
- 'Three hundred red roses
your white shirt now carries.
Your blood stinks and oozes,
all around your scarlet sashes.
But I am no longer I,
nor is this house of mine, mine.'
- 'Let me then, at least, climb up there,
up towards the high verandas.
Let me climb, let me climb there,
up towards the green verandas.
High verandas of the moonlight,
where I hear the sound of waters.'

Now they climb, the two companions,
up there to the high veranda,
letting fall a trail of blood drops,
letting fall a trail of tears.
On the morning rooftops,
trembled, the small tin lanterns.
A thousand tambourines of crystal
wounded the light of daybreak.

Green, as I love you, greenly.
Green the wind, and green the branches.
They climbed up, the two companions.
In the mouth, the dark breezes
left there a strange flavour,
of gall, and mint, and sweet-basil.
- 'Brother, friend! Where is she, tell me,
where is she, your bitter beauty?
How often, she waited for you!
How often, she would have waited,
cool the face, and dark the tresses,
on this green veranda!'

Over the cistern's surface
the gypsy girl was rocking.
Green the flesh is, green the tresses,
with eyes of frozen silver.
An ice-ray made of moonlight
holding her above the water.

How intimate the night became,
like a little, hidden plaza.
Drunken Civil Guards were beating,
beating, beating on the door frame.
Green, as I love you, greenly.
Green the wind, and green the branches.
The dark ship on the sea,
and the horse on the mountain.

The Unfaithful Wife

So I took her to the river
thinking she was virgin,
but it seems she had a husband.
It was the night of Saint Iago,
and it almost was a duty.
The lamps went out,
the crickets lit up.
By the last street corners
I touched her sleeping breasts,
and they suddenly had opened
like the hyacinth petals.
The starch
of her slip crackled
in my ears like silk fragments
ripped apart by ten daggers.
The tree crowns
free of silver light are larger,
and a horizon, of dogs, howls
far away from the river.

Past the hawthorns,
the reeds, and the brambles,
below her dome of hair
I made a hollow in the sand.
I took off my tie.

She took off a garment.
I my belt with my revolver.
She four bodices.
Creamy tuberoses
or shells are not as smooth as
her skin was, or, in the moonlight,
crystals shining brilliantly.

Her thighs slipped from me
like fish that are startled,
one half full of fire,
one half full of coldness.
That night I galloped
on the best of roadways,
on a mare of nacre,
without stirrups, without bridle.
As a man I cannot tell you
the things she said to me.
The light of understanding
has made me most discreet.
Smeared with sand and kisses,
I took her from the river.
The blades of the lilies
were fighting with the air.

I behaved as what I am,
as a true gypsy.
I gave her a sewing basket,

big, with straw-coloured satin.
I did not want to love her,
for though she had a husband
she said she was a virgin
when I took her to the river.

Gacela of Unexpected Love

No one understood the perfume
of the shadow magnolia of your belly.
No one knew you crushed completely
a humming-bird of love between your teeth.

There slept a thousand little Persian horses
in the moonlight plaza of your forehead,
while, for four nights, I embraced there
your waist, the enemy of snowfall.

Between the plaster and the jasmines,
your gaze was a pale branch, seeding.
I tried to give you, in my breastbone,
the ivory letters that say *ever*.

Ever, ever: garden of my torture,
your body, flies from me forever,
the blood of your veins is in my mouth now,
already light-free for my death.

Casida de la Rosa

The rose was
not looking for the morning:
on its branch, almost immortal,
it looked for something other.

The rose was
not looking for wisdom, or for shadow:
the edge of flesh and dreaming,
it looked for something other.

The rose was
not looking for the rose, was
unmoving in the heavens:
it looked for something other.

Casida of the Dark Doves

Through the laurel branches
I saw two doves of darkness.
The one it was the sun,
the other one was lunar.
I said: ‘Little neighbours
where is my tombstone?’
‘In my tail-feathers,’ the sun said.
‘In my throat,’ said the lunar.
And I who was out walking
with the earth wrapped round me,
saw two eagles made of white snow,
and a girl who was naked.
And the one was the other,
and the girl, she was neither.
I said: ‘Little eagles,
where is my tombstone?’
‘In my tail-feathers,’ the sun said.
‘In my throat,’ said the lunar.
Through the branches of laurel,
I saw two doves, both naked.
And the one was the other,
and the two of them were neither.

'Ay voz secreta del amor oscuro!'

O secret voice of hidden love!
O bleating without wool! O wound!
O dry camellia, bitter needle!
O sea-less current, wall-less city!

O night immense with sharpened profile,
heavenly mountain, narrow valley!
O dog inside the heart, voice going,
endless silence, full-blown iris!

Let me be, hot voice of icebergs,
and do not ask me to vanish
in weeds, where sky and flesh are fruitless.

Leave my hard ivory skull forever,
have pity on me. Stop the torture!
O I am love, O I am nature!

Every Song

Every song
is the remains
of love.

Every light
the remains
of time.
A knot
of time.

And every sigh
the remains
of a cry.

About the author

Larry Sawyer is the author of *Vertigo Diary* (BlazeVox) and also *Unable to Fully California* (Otoliths Press). He has curated the Myopic Poetry Series in Chicago since 2005 and is also the co-director of The Chicago School of Poetics (www.chicagoschoolofpoetics.com).

www.ingramcontent.com/pod-product-compliance
Ingram Content Group UK Ltd.
Pitfield, Milton Keynes, MK11 3LW, UK
UKHW041836200726
13854UKWH00003BA/1162